AF789873

Aboriginal Land Rights, the Law, and Empowerment

THE FAILURE OF ECONOMIC THEORY AS A CRITIQUE OF LAND RIGHTS

Sean Sexton

North Australia Research Unit

DISCUSSION PAPER NO. 3/1996

$10.-

First published in Australia in 1996 by the North Australia Research Unit, National Centre for Development Studies, Research School of Asian and Pacific Studies, The Australian National University.

The views expressed in this publication are those of the author and not necessarily those of the North Australia Research Unit, The Australian National University.

© North Australia Research Unit
The Australian National University, 1996

This book is copyright. Apart from any fair dealing for the purpose of private study, research, criticism or review, as permitted under the Copyright Act, no part of this publication may be reproduced by any process whatsoever without the written permission of the publisher.

National Library of Australia

Cataloguing-in-Publication entry:

Sexton, S.

Bibliography.

ISSN 1327-4791

ISBN 0 7315 2494 2

North Australia Research Unit
The Australian National University

The North Australia Research Unit (NARU) was established in 1973 — a time when The Australian National University (ANU) itself was fairly youthful. NARU is primarily a research and academic support base. The Unit's frontier days are as much a part of the history of northern Australia as they are of the history of The Australian National University and this is what gives NARU its unique status within the rest of the Australian university network.

NARU occupies a relatively large site — 4 hectares within a 10 kilometre drive from the centre of Darwin — with boundaries contiguous with the more recently developed Northern Territory University. Since opening its door to the north, NARU has expanded its portals into a modern, well resourced complex with strong links to universities, indigenous communities and a continuing political and economic focus on regional issues relevant to the top end. NARU provides an outlet for research through a successful public seminar series and through general academic publications. The Unit's own publications include a discussion paper series and, over the years, a number of well known authors have published their monographs through NARU. Also, the Unit's library specialises in northern issues — NARU expertise has become known to many researchers over the years.

Physically located in the remote top end of Australia, NARU has been something of a frontier research post but, in terms of its scholarly output, it has a record of academic research which is anything but remote. The aggregate of scholars over the years, and even today, is a reflection of the interdiciplinary nature of the people who have carried out their research while based at the Unit.

A large chunk of that research has focused on the Aboriginal and Torres Strait Islander peoples of Australia and on the social, cultural, political, economic and development issues which are part of northern Australia. The range of research projects which are underway at any particular time depend very much on the priorities of the individuals who are engaged in the actual research. Aboriginal and Torres Strait Islander issues are of continuing importance in northern Australia and, consequently, to NARU. The reasons for this would be obvious to anyone who visits northern Australia — outside of Darwin, indigenous people comprise the majority of the population in the north.

The academic content of NARU is, of course, its central purpose and, presently, there are five ANU academics on staff and several visitors from other universities. NARU offers its services to a small number of university graduate students who require a base in the north. The students are from universities around Australia and their research reflects the cross-disciplinary nature of NARU itself. Student research is supported wherever possible by the academics at NARU and by the Unit's administrative contingent. Like many other centres at the ANU in Canberra,

NARU regularly publishes academic research which has particular relevance to the Unit's work.

In 1995, NARU underwent some restructuring within the Institute of Advanced Studies at the ANU, and now comes within the jurisdiction of the National Centre for Development Studies (NCDS) which, itself, remains a key part of the Research School of Pacific and Asian Studies. From a research perspective, the shift to NCDS reflects an additional strengthening of the emphasis on the nature of relationships between traditional institutions and the political and economic structure of modern governance — particularly from a public policy perspective.

NARU's close alignments with the main campus of The Australian National University are extended not only through the coterie of research networks but through civic outreach activities. Civic outreach is important to every tertiary institution but perhaps, because of the distance — including the distance between the political culture of the north and the Canberra culture — between the ANU in Canberra and NARU, there is an added imperative to keep all channels open.

Guidelines for contributors

Papers should not exceed ten thousand words. The Harvard system of referencing is recommended, and footnotes, rather than endnotes is preferable. The styling method of this paper can be used as a guide. Authors are requested to send three copies of their paper and one copy on disk to Publications, North Australia Research Unit, PO Box 41321, Casuarina, NT 0811. Please include an abstract and short profile of the author. All enquiries regarding sales should be addressed to:

Publications
North Australia Research Unit
PO Box 41321
Casuarina
NT 0811
ph: 08 8922 0066
fax: 08 8922 0055
email: Publish.NARU@anu.edu.au

Forewarning and acknowledgements

In a recent article (Sexton 1996), I put forward the proposition that neo classical economic theory, when applied to labour law and land rights law, has the effect of reducing the empowerment and protection derived from those laws, because economic analysis does not readily incorporate these factors into definitions of 'efficiency'. This work was completed in April 1996. Between then and now, I have been on two land rights related journeys into central Australia. In addition, there has been the continuation of vexing negotiations at Century Zinc, several Court and Native Title Tribunal decisions, and the emerging proposals to amend the Native Title Act. Also, some of the discussion in the original piece had begun to crystallise into (hopefully) deeper understandings. This paper expands on the original work, and brings it up to August 1996.

I must now thank a few people: Marita Foley, Kitty Permella, and Mr Krinkle, for love and inspiration; Carol Davies and Justice Gray for patience and lessons in grammar; Dr Deborah Bird Rose for encouragement and further inspiration; The North Australia Research Unit, for providing a stream of high quality output, crucial to my survival as an undergraduate; my family, and clan Foley; Joanne Murphy, and the *Aboriginal Law Bulletin*, for making something to look forward to.

Not least of all, I must also thank indigenous people across the continent. To them I owe an enormous debt.

Aboriginal Land Rights, the Law, and Empowerment

THE FAILURE OF ECONOMIC THEORY AS A CRITIQUE OF LAND RIGHTS

Sean Sexton*

Introduction

This paper concentrates on the relationship between land rights, economic theory and power. In doing so, I am not seeking to attribute as the sole explanation of the configuration of native title legislation to neo classical economics (or economic rationalism). What I will be arguing is that economic commentary on land rights follows a particular course, which if implemented in the law, produces an inevitable outcome for indigenous groups. Some of what is written here will be known to native title stakeholders. The purpose of this discussion is to offer a critique of economic appraisal, and demonstrate what can occur when law is either unconsciously or consciously, subtly or overtly, influenced by neo classical theory.

I also want to bring to the discussion a sense of what law means in a cross cultural setting, from the perspective of a lawyer. If a particular legal

* Sean Sexton is Associate to His Honour, Justice Gray, who is a Judge of the Federal Court of Australia, the Industrial Relations Court of Australia, the Aboriginal Land Commissioner, and the Deputy President of the National Native Title Tribunal. The views expressed here are those of the author.

instrument is examined closely, the symbolism and control gained from such a law, can give an indication of how closely such laws fit with indigenous Law. It also shows how issues such as levels of education, concerns about the spiritual realm and intergenerational questions, are inextricably linked to the law's perceived success or failure. What I am describing in this paper in one sense is law's ability to recognise cultural difference. Law that relates to indigenous people must be designed so that spiritual, intergenerational, environmental, educational, and resource concerns are recognised.

The point I wish to make in this discussion is that under the *Aboriginal Land Rights (Northern Territory) Act* 1976 (Cwlth), certain mechanisms are in place that when examined closely provide power and associated benefits that seem to allow Aboriginal people to control development on terms that recognise institutional factors such as levels of education; geographical factors such as distance, difficult terrain; time and resource constraints; previous contact with mining development. These are in addition to spiritual matters such as the connection to country.

When compared to the *Native Title Act* 1993, it is apparent that compromises have been made. As the discussion progresses, it will become clear that some of the changes made for native title were made in the name of achieving greater efficiency. What I want to bring into focus is that these efficiencies are achieved by removing or diluting mechanisms present in the Land Rights Act. In removing such mechanisms, there must be some doubt about the ability of the Native Title Act to recognise cultural difference.

Siobhan McKenna (1995) makes a comparison from an economic perspective between the Land Rights Act and the Native Title Act. McKenna's conclusion is that the Native Title Act represents an economically more efficient piece of legislation. Such analysis examines law from the perspective of how such laws impede the operation of the market. I will argue that the weakness in such an appraisal of land rights legislation lies in the failure of economic analysis to acknowledge the protective and empowering functions of law. In any analysis the need to probe the deeper meaning and functions of law is crucial.

In this context a link between economic analysis of labour law and land rights legislation can be made. By making the link the common failure of economic critique of land rights and labour law is made clear. The inability to acknowledge empowerment and protection as having a legitimate place in the market, and the inability to acknowledge the need for law to provide such protection (largely because the 'market' is unable to do so, or alternatively, because a level of protection will be rationally derived by market operation), means that law reform driven by economic rationalist critique may produce negative social outcomes. I will put the view that law must be analysed for who it empowers and protects. On this basis, the Land Rights Act retains its status as the superior land rights legislation in Australia. This conclusion is based on what I discuss below, namely, that the Land Rights Act is able to recognise and accept cultural difference and historical disadvantage, and provide mechanisms that bridge gaps in power and resources.

To illustrate the hypothesis, I will use the provisions governing exploration and mining as a case study which will show how economic theory impacts land rights legislation. In doing so, the 'costs' identified by economic theory are deconstructed to show what these mechanisms mean to indigenous people. The inefficiencies identified by economic theory are most often devices that protect and empower indigenous people. From this, it will become clear that to remove such mechanisms inevitably means that outcomes for indigenous people will almost certainly be negative under the Native Title Act. The likelihood of this being so is strengthened by data which suggests that labour law fashioned in the neo-classical mould invariably produces negative outcomes for employees.

The use of labour law in comparison with land rights law may also provide some inspiration for strategy. Unions and other peak employee organisations have developed techniques for dealing with law shaped by neo classical theory. Collective agreements and accords appear to have some elements in common with Regional Agreements negotiated between competing land users. The enforceability of these agreements may at some stage be questioned. The treatment by Courts of such agreements in labour law could well be instructive. Other strategic behaviour undertaken by land councils has broad similarities with trade union activity. The pitfalls and advantages gained by such tactics could again be instructive for native title parties.

Practical considerations aside, I wish to focus on understanding the nature of the economic critique of law. With this in hand, some sense of what the Native Title Act can and cannot deliver, and why, will begin to emerge. Recent decisions of the Federal Court, and the National Native Title Tribunal provide insights into the largely unresolved tension between indigenous and non-indigenous aspirations for land and waters.

Law and economic theory — the labour law hypothesis

In the field of labour/industrial relations, the most economically efficient system involves direct bargaining between employers and employees. The market will take care of employee protection, and exploitation is unlikely to take place (Fischel 1984: 1068). Such a view significantly underestimates the power imbalance that exists between employer and employee (Kahn-Freund 1972: 8). It is also inconsistent with the constant struggle by labour with capital for improvements in pay and conditions. It also does not sit well with the labour practices we see in unprotected markets.

Market-driven labour practices contrast sharply with much of the law and policy that has developed in Australia. Employees have managed to extract significant advances in working conditions through a combination of collective action and protective legislation. Features of Australian labour law include centralised wage control, recognition of unions, unlawful termination legislation, and regulation of the work environment (occupational health and safety) offer empowerment to employees.

The protective function that labour law fulfils is either expressly or implicitly a recognition of the power imbalance between employer and employee. It is also a recognition of the need to regulate in these circumstances, based largely on the realities of labour markets across the world. Despite the large body of empirical evidence available that supports the need for such laws, there is opposition to the imposition of protective regimes. Protective labour laws are harshly criticised by economic analysis, because they generate obstacles for the path of market forces (Fischel 1984, and Sharad 1996: 2). The economic appraisal of labour law centres around the identification of these obstacles as 'transaction costs'. A market is operating most efficiently when these costs are lowest.

Economic critique of labour law has been both influential and persuasive. During the terms of successive federal Labor governments there have been significant changes in labour laws that include the movement away from centralised wage control (Bureau of Industry Economics 1996), introduction of voluntary unionism, and reductions in workers' compensation benefits (Robinson 1994). The most radical reforms have occurred in Australian States (Mitchell & Naughton 1993). It is likely that the recently elected conservative government will attempt to pass legislation that is similar in character. In New Zealand, labour law created in the free market image was introduced in 1991. This scheme is much closer to the 'ideal' system of labour regulation

(Churchman 1991). It represents a fundamental shift in the direction of labour law, and it is no coincidence that such schemes offer lower protection to employees. The move to reduce the cost of bargaining with employees is driven by economic theory striving for the most efficient outcome. I will now show that in the context of striking bargains with indigenous people, the desire to achieve an outcome involving the lowest possible cost is also evident when the Native Title Act is compared to the Land Rights Act. To achieve such a goal, features prominent in the Land Rights Act are either not found in the Native Title Act or are substantially weakened.

The economics of land rights — consent to explore and mine

The Land Rights Act

An economic appraisal of the Native Title Act and the Land Rights Act, as in the case for labour law, centres around the need to identify and reduce 'transaction costs'. Under the model followed by McKenna, these are the costs of consultation, compliance with the law, and of identifying those to be consulted. It is, however, no coincidence that just as in labour law, these costs are often found to be the devices that offer empowerment and protection.

A crucial mechanism in the Land Rights Act is the consent provisions (the 'veto'), that regulate exploration and mining, and are discussed in some detail by McKenna (1995a: 301–5). The veto provisions require mining companies to present a reasonable proposal to Aboriginal people, and the capacity to either accept or reject that proposal. Such a degree of control has never previously been a feature of relations between indigenous people and mining companies in Australia (Roberts 1978, and Connell & Howitt 1991).

It is important to understand what the veto contains in the way of power and protection. Rather than simply being a device to which people can say 'yes' or 'no' to exploration and mining, it is a bundle of interconnected devices that allocate power and cultural validation. Deconstructing the bundle shows that consciously or unconsciously, the veto is a mechanism that allows indigenous people to affirm the connection that they may have to land or waters. The capacity to withhold consent to exploration and mining is also a key aspect of self-determination for Aboriginal communities. The consent provisions give people the time to consider applications, and insulation from the pressure of developers and governments eager to see projects move swiftly. In essence, these provisions allow Aboriginal people to be *included* in the negotiations, and have *control* over how development is shaped.

The uniqueness and the power of the consent provisions has not gone unnoticed by the mining sector. Calls for change were successful, when in 1987 amendments were passed that altered the nature of the consent. Prior to 1987, consent had to be obtained at both the exploration and the extraction phase of a mining proposal. This disjunctive procedure was seen as inefficient (McKenna 1995a: 303) and a significant disincentive to invest in mining in the Northern Territory.

The 1987 amendments mean that Aboriginal people must at the exploration phase provide a once only consent. Aboriginal people must envisage a fully fledged mining operation before a single hole is drilled in the ground during exploration. McKenna says that Land Councils, the statutory representatives of Aboriginal people in the Northern Territory, have reduced the expected benefits of the amended procedures by insisting on the production of detailed proposals. Firstly, such details are a function of compliance with the Land Rights Act, and secondly, how can an informed decision be made without detailed information? The amendments, inspired by the promise of greater efficiency, lead to the situation where both sides must negotiate from positions of uncertainty. Inevitably this will increase the cost of bargaining. As McKenna states, one exploration project in a thousand reaches the extraction phase (1995a: 303). Under the amendments, each proposal must come with a detailed vision of the fruits of exploration. The costs incurred in exploration under the Land Rights Act are *necessary* to provide both protection from exploitation and the making of informed decisions.

I argue that it is a mistake to view the veto in one dimension only. It is much more than a potentially disruptive 'yes' or 'no' authority. The cross cultural dimension is lost in this simplistic analysis. This is borne out by those who describe the veto as a lock-up of potential wealth. The ability to go beyond the text of the law, and see what Aboriginal people are able to draw from such a law is crucial to an understanding of development in a cross cultural setting. As I will show below, the consent provisions (the 1987 amendments notwithstanding) of the Land Rights Act were drafted with the clear intention of providing power to Aboriginal people. Before that, however, I will now discuss the operation of the 'equivalent' provisions in the Native Title Act. I will argue that whilst empowerment is contemplated in the Native Title Act, it is also very conscious of the interests of development.

The Native Title Act

Pressure from the mining sector, influenced by economic critique, and the need to reduce transaction costs, led to the Native Title Act being passed without consent provisions similar to the Land Rights Act. The absence of veto in the Native Title Act is not an accident of legal drafting. What the Native Title Act provides is "the right to negotiate" (ss.26–44), where mining interests seeking to undertake activity on land subject to a native title claim, negotiate with those claimants. There is no veto. If the parties are unable to make an agreement, the parties go to an arbitral body (the National Native Title Tribunal) and have the matter resolved (s.35).

At this point in time, future Act determinations have been few in number. The determinations published thus far raise some interesting points about the nature of exploration and mining leases in Western Australia. They would be familiar to those versed in the Land Rights Act. Negotiation commences when the grantee party seeks an exploration licence from which a mining lease can then be granted. A three-member National Native Title Tribunal panel found that in Western Australia, there is considerable uncertainty during the negotiating process (National Native Title Tribunal 1996(e)).

> The dilemma is, how can the Tribunal sensibly address the criteria in s.39 and make a determination when it does not know what rights, beyond exploration, might be exercised over the next 42 years or even what will be the nature and extent of exploration activity? (National Native Title Tribunal 1996(e): 131).

In two determinations, both by three-member panels, the issue of whether conditions could be imposed at both the exploration phase and the mining phase was raised. Onc panel concluded that there was only one opportunity for the Tribunal to impose conditions, and this was likely to be at the exploration stage of a project (National Native Title Tribunal 1996(d)). A second panel considered the implications of a two stage process before concluding that the Native Title Act did not expressly state either way that a two-stage process was within the power of the Tribunal (National Native Title Tribunal 1996(e)). This controversy over a conjunctive or disjunctive process surfaced in the Land Rights Act with the 1987 amendments. Miners must come with a vision of the extraction phase. Under the Native Title Act the uncertainty of bargaining when so much is unknown, highlights the fact that a two-stage process has considerable merit for both miners and indigenous communities. After exploration, the prospects for mining will become much clearer, and with a proven deposit, miners will be in position to devote the resources required to design the extraction phase, and explain it to indigenous people. If the Tribunal find making a determination difficult under these circumstances, then how are indigenous communities expected to manage the negotiations, facing difficulties which will be exacerbated by cultural differences, time, and resource constraints? It is also worth noting that on the 'Neate' panel (National Native Title Tribunal 1996(e)), the grantee party (the potential explorer) could offer little in the way of detailed plans for a mine. How could they, since they do not know what is there to mine?

The right to negotiate process is seen as making the granting of exploration and mining licences simpler and cheaper than the Land Rights Act (McKenna 1995a: 309). This may be the case, but it is because the empowering and protective mechanism of the consent has been removed. However, negotiating from a position of uncertainty is likely to increase the costs of striking agreements in the same manner as the post 1987 Land Rights Act.

The catch-cry of simplicity and cost efficiency is a hallmark of economic critique, and is also used to justify reforms to labour law. The right to negotiate places native title holders in a weaker bargaining position than those who enjoy the protection of the Land Rights Act. However, other provisions in the Native Title Act further weaken the bargaining position of indigenous people.

Expedited procedures

Within the Native Title Act are provisions for acts that may attract the expedited procedure (ss.29, 237). These acts are excluded from the right to negotiate framework. It was generally felt that few applications for mining exploration would attract this 'fast track'. Indigenous groups expected that few mining exploration could be classified as activity that attracts the 'fast track', primarily because of the creation of the 'right to negotiate procedures' (Allbrook 1995: 99, and Aboriginal and Torres Strait Islander Social Justice Commission 1995: 148–9). Under this process, a 'government party' declares that it believes that a particular act, such as an exploration licence is an act attracting the expedited procedure. Indigenous communities are then given an opportunity to object to the proposal. The time frame for objection is two months (s.29). A successful objection must satisfy a test which examines disruption to community life, sites of significance, and disruption to land and waters (s.237). For many communities and their representatives, it is a formidable task to deal with the influx of applications, with significant logistical and resource availability hurdles to overcome (Allbrook 1995: 98). This is particularly the case in Western Australia, where the majority of exploration applications are being channelled through the expedited procedure. The time limits, which are said to be positive economic attributes, are more a function of keeping project realisation time to a minimum than they are about protecting the interests of indigenous communities. The time limits described by the then Prime Minister, Paul Keating, as tight but fair (Keating 1993: 2080), also underestimate the need to consider properly the implications of the proposals, and the resource and geographical constraints that many communities must face.

Further doubts about the protective qualities of the Native Title Act are raised by the interpretation of the expedited provisions by the National Native Title Tribunal. In the course of hearing several objections to the expedited procedure, Tribunal Deputy President Paul Seaman has made the disturbance test difficult for indigenous communities to satisfy (National Native Title Tribunal 1995, *re: Irruntju-Papalankuntja Community*, and National Native Title Tribunal 1996a, *re: Nyungah People*).

The trend in the interpretation of the expedited procedure has seen three decisions of the Tribunal go before the Federal Court, seeking a review of the Tribunal decisions (Federal Court of Australia 1996, *Ben Ward and Others v Western Australia and Others*, Decision No. 334/96). In a limited sense, the result of this case represents a breakthrough for indigenous people. Justice Carr found that the Tribunal had erred in law in finding that 'direct interference' with community life [s.237(a) Native Title Act], necessarily meant only physical interference (pp.26–30). The word 'physical' interference does not form part of the Native Title Act. It is reasoning that demonstrates that His Honour is conscious of the non physical nature of the relationship of indigenous people to land. In finding that the Tribunal erred in law by way of its narrow construction, the scope for obtaining a successful objection to an expedited act may now be widened. These cases have been remitted back to the Tribunal for reconsideration of the issue of 'direct interference', and are discussed below.

However, His Honour rejected the remaining grounds of appeal against the three Tribunal decisions. These grounds included an attempt to shift the burden of proof from claimants to those seeking to activate the expedited procedure; a challenge to the construction of the expression 'major disturbance'; a challenge to the effectiveness of Western Australian heritage protection legislation, which was accepted by the Tribunal as adequate; and that the interpretation of the expedited procedure was in fact inconsistent with the objects of the Native Title Act. The applicants in this case put the view that the Native Title Act is meant to be empowering, or in legal terms, beneficial legislation. It is difficult to reconcile the notion of a fast track process operating within a framework that is meant to be inclusive, and empowering, particularly when there is a process already in place that deals with exploration and mining (Aboriginal and Torres Strait Islander Social Justice Commission 1995: 148–9).

Following the decision of Justice Carr, the indications are that a successful objection on the grounds of 'direct interference' may be easier to sustain, which is a positive step for indigenous communities. National Native Title Tribunal Member Sumner has found in all but one of the cases reviewed in the Federal Court by Justice Carr, that the expedited procedure did not apply (National Native Title Tribunal 1996(b)). In arriving at theses conclusions, Sumner suggests that anxiety or unease about development impacts may constitute 'direct interference' (National Native Title Tribunal 1996(b): 9). Sustaining an objection to an application under the expedited procedure injects a measure of control over exploration and mining, as negotiations towards an agreement can now commence, within the right to negotiate framework.

In the matter before Member Sumner, submissions made by the native title party give a real insight into what is at stake for many indigenous people.

> 13. In the past mining companies and others have not asked permission of the Miriuwung-Gajerrong people and have messed up sacred places. This happened when the bottom dam (Kununurra diversion dam) and the top dam (Lake Argyle dam) were built. When these dams were built a lot of the old people felt sorry for their country and the Miriuwung-Gajerrong people believe that because of this a lot of the old people died.
>
> 14. It is the view of the Miriuwung-Gajerrong people that when mining companies do not ask permission to come into their country it shows that they have no respect for their culture. According to law and custom it is breaking their law if dreaming tracks are messed up. Also if these dreaming tracks are messed up then they believe that all the animals and plants might disappear.

> Because of the dreaming tracks running through the country the Miriuwung-Gajerrong people want to sign an agreement with the mining company for a Ngarrangani (site) survey before they start digging or drilling (National Native Title Tribunal 1996(b): 13).

Earlier in the discussion, I attempted to describe the nature of the Land Rights Act consent provisions — the submissions quoted above encapsulate much of this description. The crucial elements are control, abidance by indigenous Law, and the inseparable nature of land and people. The respect for cultural difference, and the need to be included, are significantly underestimated in the haste to explore outside the right to negotiate framework.

In view of how the consent provisions operate under the Native Title Act, it is worth considering what Justice Woodward, in his Second Land Rights report, said on the issue of consenting to exploration and mining:

> I believe that to deny to Aborigines the right to prevent mining on their land is to deny the reality of their land rights (Woodward 1974: 108).

For Woodward, the protective and empowering function of land rights legislation was fundamental to his understanding of the needs and aspirations of indigenous people. He understood that the special nature of indigenous relationships to land, and the degree to which they were unable to control mining on their land, warranted such protection. The empowerment and protection that a veto offers is simply not available under the Native Title Act, and the operation of its replacement 'the right to negotiate' and the expedited procedure, cast doubt on the ability of the legislation to fulfil the aspirations of indigenous people. It may well be the case that transaction costs are reduced, but the costs are transferred to indigenous people. These are the people who have least power to trade, the least ground to give. Indeed, some communities who remain 'landless' (whilst claims are being heard) have no ground to give. Obliged to pay for the creation of the Australian nation with their land and lives, indigenous communities are now forced to accept legislation that is steeped in compromise. The language of the former prime minister in the second reading speech is telling.

> Industry gains a great deal from this Bill because it imposes clear, statutory rules for land use where the Mabo decision left uncertainty. The Bill does not

> lock land away. On the contrary, as I explained, we are not setting up complicated barriers to mining exploration or operations (Keating 1993: 2081).

Giving indigenous communities due regard to their relationship to land, implementing the principles of self determination, becomes, by implication, a complicated barrier to exploration and mining. Despite protests to the contrary, the operation of the Native Title Act in the area of gaining consent to explore and mine, should be of significant comfort to those who endorse the economic critiques of the Land Rights Act. The veto power of the Land Rights Act is effectively neutralised under the Native Title Act. However, in taking this course, some of the lessons of the Land Rights Act have not been learnt. The promise of a once only consent being more efficient is shadowed by uncertainty, and the National Native Title Tribunal is now encountering similar difficulties under the Native Title Act. The real difference between the two laws is that under the Land Rights Act, Aboriginal people have a clear 'yes' or 'no' authority, which as I have discussed previously, is linked to the relationship with land, and self determination. Having such a power compels mining companies to advance their thinking on the impacts of their proposals on the landscape and its people.

Direct negotiations

McKenna reports that another transaction cost that could be reduced under native title is the removal of the monopoly on land council representation that the Land Rights Act imposes (McKenna 1995b: 11). In a similar vein, economic critique of the union movement describe trade unions as a mechanism by which employees establish a monopoly on their labour (Fischel 1984: 1071). Such a monopoly as exists in the Land Rights Act is not present in the Native Title Act. Indigenous communities under the Native Title Act are in principle free to choose their representatives. The land council monopoly is absent from the Native Title Act, largely due to the resource sector, using economic theory to label such a mechanism as 'inefficient' (Aboriginal and Torres Strait Islander Social Justice Commission 1995: 65). I acknowledge here that support for land councils in the Northern Territory and elsewhere, is not universal amongst Aboriginal communities, and that some prefer to have the option of choosing their own representatives.

Just as the promise of greater efficiencies in gaining consents under the amended Land Rights Act have not been realised, the lack of a monopoly on representation has caused significant problems for intending miners (Macleay 1996). The regulatory monopoly by Northern Territory land councils under the Land RightsAct, operate as 'one-stop shops', liaising between indigenous people and miners (Altman 1995: 8).

The difficulties in finding negotiating parties (one of the fundamental types of transaction costs identified by economists), much lamented in the current controversy over the Century Zinc mine in Queensland, could be resolved to a large degree by legitimising the presence of the local land council in the negotiations (and accepting for better or worse, the results of their representation). Having an appointed voice for indigenous people means that the mining company knows who they are talking to. The current situation lends itself to confusion because there is uncertainty about exactly who should be talking to whom, and who can speak for whom. Far from being efficient, it leads to the situation seen during the attempts to negotiate at Century Zinc. Not surprisingly, there are now calls from the resource sector to grant such monopolies under the Native Title Act (Macleay 1996). The 'one stop shop' approach follows the argument that supports the involvement of trade unions in the process of bargaining. Identifiable, well resourced, experienced players negate the need for potentially costly individual negotiations.

Closely linked to the push for the removal of land council monopolies is the call for the introduction of face to face negotiations between traditional owners and mining companies (McKenna 1995a: 307). It is remarkably similar to the calls to abandon collective agreements and replace them with individual employment contracts, negotiated between employer and employee on a one-on-one basis.

There are strong arguments against face to face negotiations between indigenous people and mining companies. Statistically, it is shown that indigenous people are amongst the poorest of the poor (in material terms) in this country (Australian Bureau of Statistics 1995). Indicators of education, health, and financial status show us that frequently indigenous people are the most disempowered in our society (Australian Bureau of Statistics 1995). It would rarely be the case that such negotiations would be conducted by people other than the highly educated and articulate team selected for the task, and in a language other than English. Land councils, like unions, serve to even up the balance of power. They provide insulation from the pressures of commercial interests eager to pursue a particular project. To use economic argument to remove land councils and unions from the picture is often merely a mask used to deny access to the crucial functions that these organisations perform. The history of indigenous people's exposure to mining companies in Australia (Roberts 1978 and Connell & Howitt 1991) and the world-wide experiences of employees show us that the 'market' is not benign to their interests. The landscape of the Australian continent is littered with examples of the 'market' operating in an unfettered manner (see Annabell 1977 for a description of the exploration for uranium in the Northern Territory).

Once again, just as the veto is not simply a 'yes' or 'no' device, the role of land councils is underpinned by empowerment and protection. Without resorting to an exhaustive deconstruction of the functions of land councils, it is sufficient to say that councils play an intermediary role similar to trade unions. It is a powerful and crucial role that they both fulfil. It seems unimaginably crude for economic theory to suggest that by taking land councils out of the picture, transactions across cultural barriers will be simply more efficient. They also have the potential to be transactions that are unjust, and ignorant of many of the values held by indigenous communities. The lessons learnt from the Land Rights Act by anthropologists and lawyers should be learnt also by economic commentators. The move to freedom of representative choice leads potentially to uncertainty and chaos, and the possibility of exposure to negotiations conducted from uninformed or weak bargaining positions. Unless the Native Title Act is changed, and land councils given a role similar to that provided for in the Land Rights Act, we can expect more of the uncertainty and angst experienced by all concerned at Century Zinc. Far from being an economic liability, the monopoly enjoyed by land councils under the Land Rights Act provides a sensible mixture of certainty and protection. It is another example of the need for economic theory to actively engage the wider context of a subject undergoing economic scrutiny. An understanding of the workings of the Land Rights Act (particularly on the specific issue of land council representation), beyond the economic realm is crucial to any meaningful economic appraisal.

What the comparison between the Land Rights Act and Native Title Act, and the link to labour law tells us

The link that economic theory provides between labour law and land rights is important for two reasons. First, it shows how the analysis of a law pursuing protective or empowering function is significantly different to one that looks from the perspective of how much that law impedes the operation of the market. Second, it shows that when economic critique influences the law, protective mechanisms are removed, or reduced in scope. This is because the 'costs' that are identified contain meaning and symbolism that is either misunderstood or ignored by economic theory.

There is considerable evidence to suggest that labour law born of neo-classical economics is not able to advance the position of employees. The results of surveys show that in New Zealand, under the *Employment Contracts Act* levels of job satisfaction, security and trust are very low, and that there have been measurable effects on wealth distribution and wage outcomes (Hince & Harbridge 1994: 252). In Australia, a similar picture is painted, even though at this point in time, the labour law reforms (at a Federal level at least) have not been as radical as those in New Zealand (Department of Industrial Relations 1995). In Australia, it is suggested that occupational health and safety outcomes are being traded off in the enterprise bargaining process, and that (for employees) occupational health and safety is compromised by the inadequate bargaining capacities of employees (Heiler 1995). The experience in the United Kingdom is that the Thatcher reforms have led to sectors of low union membership, and have higher levels of turnover, dismissal, and workplace injury (Hince & Harbridge 1994: 252). The shift in bargaining power caused by the removal of protective legislation, produces these results.

Can a general principle be derived?

It seems plausible to argue that a methodology that produces discernible shifts in power in one legal realm will then tend to be the same in another. One cannot, however, assume that simply because labour law informed by measures of neo-classical theory produces negative results for employees, then a neo-classical native title law will do the same for indigenous people. What this discussion shows is that strong evidence does exist to support the conclusion that a land rights scheme shaped by significant reference to economic theory (in particular, neo-classical theory) will inevitably tend to produce negative outcomes for indigenous people.

Perhaps from this it is possible to glean a general principle, that neo-classical theory applied to law will produce negative results for those with least power. The principal reason being that economic theory does not take into account the empowering function of law.

The cost of power

Economic critique compels markets to journey along a path of least cost. Understandably, from this perspective, the reduction of transaction costs is a most desirable goal. However, as this discussion shows, these 'costs' are often found to be the devices from which those without power derive it. When the fundamental nature of the so-called market impediments is inadequately understood, any attempt to make land rights 'cost lowest' must mean that protective mechanisms will be removed. This is clear from the above comparisons between the Land Rights Act and the Native Title Act.

Empowerment and protection are legitimate expectations of law. It is also legitimate to expect that an economic analysis of law recognise these functions. As the labour law example shows, inequity can result if efficiency is given priority over empowerment. Land rights legislation must have some impact on development if it is to empower and protect indigenous people. In other words, the costs incurred in doing business with indigenous communities may exceed the costs incurred in the wider community, but that these costs reflect the nature of the indigenous relationship to land, the existing inequities in the allocation of bargaining power, the availability of resources, and geographical factors.

The expectation that costs will be of a certain magnitude, all the time, regardless of the context in which a project is placed, is unrealistic. Costs may be contained within certain preconceived limits in commercial settings, but in the case of dealing with indigenous communities, the cross cultural differences must be understood. In other words, consider what these 'costs' are. They are the costs of giving indigenous people the time and space within which they make decisions that may have implications for many generations.

What I am in essence describing, is the conflict between indigenous and European land ethics. When land is inseparable from the person, as it is for many indigenous people, normal market principles, premised on European concepts of 'property', where land is a tradeable commodity, cannot be so easily applied. McKenna states that if indigenous people value the land associated with a mining proposal more than the miners, then it should remain in indigenous hands (1995b: 20). Such a view is at odds with her appraisal of the Native Title Act. It is the reduction of the transaction costs that makes it more difficult than ever for land to remain in indigenous hands. The arbitration of future acts by the National Native Title Tribunal, the expedited procedure, and the placement of onus of proof in objection applications, are all examples of the difficulties in maintaining control over development. The costs as identified convey power to people. Removing the costs must result in the removal of power.

In addition, as the above discussion shows, predicted benefits derived from the application of classical economic theory do not always materialise. The changes in the Land Rights Act in 1987, and the potential uncertainty created by lack of defined negotiating parties, show that economic critique of land rights needs to become more acquainted with cultural realities.

Implications for the bigger picture: A moral imperative unfulfilled?

The impact of the change in focus from protection to efficiency has wider implications than the issue of mining and exploration. This discussion has already shown that the Native Title Act, like contemporary labour law, is influenced by economic theory, to an extent that is not evident in the Land Rights Act, or previous regimes of labour law in Australia. On a national level at least, the moral imperative that drove the reforms of the 1970s, following the abandonment of assimilation, remains substantially unfulfilled. A land rights law that cannot protect and empower indigenous people casts doubt on its ability to deliver meaningful self determination. The colonial grip on control of land management, loosened substantially under the Land Rights Act, is tightened under the Native Title Act. Of course, the Land Rights Act is no panacea. Large areas of country are statutorily out of reach, particularly pastoral leases. The Native Title Act has the potential at least to deliver some of this country back to its people. The flipside is that the Native Title Act does not afford the same level of power or self determination.

If native title derives from the notion that indigenous law and relationships to land and waters survived the legal fiction of *terra nullius* and colonisation, then necessarily it demands a legislative response that protects these rights. To continue to temper the rights and aspirations by reference to economic analysis that seems unable to acknowledge the need for protection and empowerment inevitably means that indigenous people will suffer further injustice.

Concluding remarks

To follow the history of labour law is to follow the rise and fall of empowering and beneficial legislation. I have argued here that it is true also of land rights legislation. For the interests of both employees and indigenous people to be advanced, we must see a shift in the way in which legal policy is generated and implemented, and also a widening of the engagement in the real contexts of peoples' lives for economic theory. In essence, what I have endeavoured to do here is to show that viewed through the window of economic theory, law can be made more efficient, but, viewed through a window that appraises law for its empowering or protective qualities, the appraisal may well be significantly different. On this basis the Land Rights Act clearly offers much to Aboriginal people in the Northern Territory when dealing with applications to explore and mine. The Native Title Act falls short of offering the kinds of protections that are enjoyed under the Land Rights Act.

Economic analysis of land rights may be methodologically sound, but in the end produces a predictable result. The Native Title Act *is* more economically efficient because some of the protective and empowering mechanisms of the Land Rights Act have been either removed or diluted. They are removed because their importance to indigenous people is not acknowledged beyond their identification as market impediments.

Finally, it must be said that mining deals continue to be struck in the Northern Territory. The Land Rights Act has not seen an end to exploration and mining. The crucial difference between the Northern Territory and laws in other jurisdictions, including the Native Title Act, is that these deals are struck against a background of a process that includes Aboriginal people, and protects them against exploitation. They work within a framework that allows indigenous people to be in firm control of both their land and their lives. For indigenous aspirations to be fulfilled, we need to be conscious of the power of law to include and protect.

We also need to understand the narrow view of law that economic theory projects, and the limitations of its methodology. To look beyond law as something that does or does not comply with market expectations, is to start to uncover much more of its meaning. When we unlock the door marked 'veto' we find that a simple 'yes' or 'no' concept becomes time and space; it becomes intergenerational; it also takes on a spiritual dimension. Economic theory must consider how cross cultural issues alter the picture. Costs currently incurred in dealing with indigenous communities under the Land Rights Act, may not be distorted and inflated as economists suggest. They may in fact be the true cost of dealing with, and respecting, cultural difference.

References

Aboriginal and Torres Strait Islander Social Justice Commissioner 1995, 'Native Title Report, July 1994-June 1995', Australian Government Publishing Service, Canberra.

Allbrook, M. 1995 'Working with the Future Act Regime', in P. Burke (ed.), *The Skills of Native Title Practice: Proceedings of a Workshop,* Australian Institute of Aboriginal and Torres Strait Islander Studies, Native Title Research Unit, Canberra.

Altman, J.C. 1995 'Native Title Act 1993: Implementation Issues for Resource Developers', Discussion Paper No. 88/1995, Centre for Aboriginal Economic Policy Research, Canberra.

Annabell, R. 1977 *The Uranium Hunters*, Rigby Ltd.

Australian Bureau of Statistics 1995 'National Aboriginal and Torres Strait Islander Survey 1994; Detailed Findings', Australian Government Publishing Service, Canberra.

Bureau of Industry Economics 1996 'Setting the Scene: Micro Reform, Impacts on Firms', Report 96/1, Australian Government Publishing Service, Canberra.

Churchman, P. 1991 'Tracing the Arc of the Pendulum: The Regulation of Collective Bargaining in New Zealand', *New Zealand Law Journal*, October, p.357.

Connell, J. & R. Howitt (eds) 1991 *Mining and Indigenous People in Australasia*, Sydney University Press, Sydney.

Department of Industrial Relations 1995 'Enterprise Bargaining in Australia: Developments under the *Industrial Relations Reform Act* 1993', Australian Government Publishing Service, Canberra.

Federal Court of Australia 1995 *Ben Ward and Others v The State of Western Australia and Australian United Gold NL; Clarrie Smith v The State of Western Australia and C.R.A. Exploration Pty. Ltd. and B.H.P. Exploration Pty. Ltd.* Unreported judgment, 14 December 1995, Federal Court of Australia, Per Lee J, Decision No. 1165/95.

Federal Court of Australia 1996 *Ben Ward and Others v The State of Western Australia and Australian United Gold NL; Clarrie Smith v The State of Western Australia and C.R.A. Exploration Pty. Ltd. and B.H.P. Exploration Pty. Ltd.* Unreported judgment, 9 May 1996, Federal Court of Australia, Per Carr J, Decision No. 334/96.

Fischel, D. 1984 'Labour Markets and Labour Law Compared with Capital Markets and Corporate Law', 51 *University of Chicago Law Review*, 1061-77.

Heiler, K. 1995 'Is Enterprise Bargaining Good For Your Health?', Australian Centre for Industrial Relations Research and Training, University of New South Wales.

Hince, K. & R. Harbridge 1994 'The *Employment Contracts Act*; An Interim Assessment', (1993-94) *New Zealand Journal of Industrial Relations*, 19(3), 235-55.

Kahn-Freund, O. 1972 *Labour and the Law*, Stevens and Sons.

Keating, P.J. 1993 Second Reading Speech, *Hansard*, House of Representatives, 16 November.

Macleay, J. 1996 'Title Fights and Ground Rules', *The Australian*, Thursday 18 April, p.27.

McKenna, S. 1995a 'Negotiating Mining Agreements under the *Native Title Act* 1993', *Agenda*, 2(3), 301-12.

McKenna, S. 1995b 'Assessing the Relative Allocative Efficiency of the *Native Title Act* 1993 and the *Aboriginal Land Rights (Northern Territory) Act* 1976', Discussion Paper No. 79/1995, Centre for Aboriginal Economic Policy Research, Canberra.

Mitchell, R. & R. Naughton 1993 'Radical Labour Law Reform and the Demise of the Victorian Industrial Relations System', *New Zealand Journal of Industrial Relations*, 275-88.

National Native Title Tribunal 1995 Re: *Irruntyju-Papulankuntja Community*, 6 October, per Deputy President Paul Seaman QC.

National Native Title Tribunal 1996a Re: *Nyungah People,* WO95/29, WO95/32, WO95/36, WO95/37, 30 April, per Deputy President Paul Seaman QC.

National Native Title Tribunal 1996b Re: *Nganawongka People and Others*, WO95/21, WO95/22, WO95/23; Re: *Miriuwung-Gajerrong People*, WO95/11, WO95/34, 26 July 1996, per Sumner CJ, Member.

National Native Title Tribunal 1996c Re: *Ngaluma and Injibandi Peoples*, WO96/17, 26 July, per Wilson K., Member.

National Native Title Tribunal 1996d Re: *Koara People*, WF96/1, WF96/5, WO96/11, 23 July, per Deputy President Paul Seaman QC, Dianne Smith, and Michael McDaniel.

National Native Title Tribunal 1996e Re: *Waljen Peoples*, WF96/3, WF96/12, 17 July, per Sumner CJ, P. O'Neil, G.Neate.

Roberts, J. 1978 *Massacres to Mining: The Colonisation of Aboriginal Australia*, Dove Communications.

Sexton, S. 1996 'Law, Empowerment, and Economic Rationalism', Aboriginal Law Bulletin, 3(81), 12-15.

Sharad, T. 1996 'Competing Models of Worker Representation — the ILO Collective Bargaining Principles and Part VIB of the *Industrial Relations Act* 1988', Centre for Employment and Labour Relations Law, Working Paper No. 10, April.

Robinson, M. 1994 'Workers Compensation in Victoria: From WorkCare to WorkCover', *Journal of Industrial Relations*, June.

Woodward, A.E. (Justice) 1974 Aboriginal Land Rights Commission: Final Report, April, Australian Government Publishing Service, Canberra.